Grace Upon Grace:

The story of Ibrahima Kodio and a remarkable school in West Africa

Brandon Pomeroy

Elpida Press
Kansas City

From God's fullness we have all received, grace upon grace.
-John 1:16

A special thank you to Sofia Pomeroy for help with editing and formatting.

Published by Elpida Press
elpidapresskc@gmail.com
Elpidapress.org

ISBN: 978-0692746066
ISBN-10: 0692746064

For all who dream of a kinder world.

Chapter 1
The Dogon, Christian Missionaries, and the Birth of a School

It is difficult to overstate how far away Grace Private School is from our lives. It's distant culturally, socioeconomically, and of course physically. Most flights to Mali go through Paris. After the overnight flight from the United States to France, and a layover that lasts from two to six hours, it's another six-hour flight to Bamako. These days most of the people on that leg are Malian, as tourism nearly completely disappeared following the March 2012 military coup. Since then, an Ebola scare, kidnappings of foreigners, hotel bombings, an Islamic terrorist group in the eastern part of the country, followed by French retaliation, have had the effect of keeping all but the most determined visitors away. Which is a shame, because like in the US or anywhere else in this beautiful, wonderful world, nearly everyone in Mali is humble, gracious, welcoming and so pleased to meet us.

Arriving in Bamako after dark, the dry smoky warm air fills one's lungs immediately upon disembarking. Six time zones and a world away from Kansas City the journey has really only begun. From the plane we crowd into a bus that absurdly takes us fifty yards across the tarmac to customs. Nodding and smiling and filling in the forms to the best of our ability we make it through to the hot and crowded baggage claim area. Sometimes Ibrahima or one of our other friends is able to get through security to help and sometimes not. Usually at least one piece of luggage doesn't make the entire journey so we go to the lost baggage office where, like similar offices everywhere, the outdated computer system and slow inefficient process keeps us stranded in the airport until well after midnight.

Koro is over four hundred and fifty miles from Bamako, the last sixty of which are on a dirt road. Even under the best conditions, with a talented driver and a well-maintained truck, it is a thirteen-hour drive. It isn't particularly safe to drive after the sun goes down. It gets *really* dark at night. Most vehicles don't have taillights and many don't have reflectors. They suddenly appear a few yards in front of the truck. There are cows and goats on the road. Bicycles and pedestrians. There are overturned trucks scattered along the highway. A recent accident with a semi on its side, its load scattered all over the shoulder and beyond, its passengers sitting on the merchandise, are still there three days later on the way back through.

So, we drive during the day. We see baobab trees, a few small hills, not many other trees but areas of fairly dense brush. I drink Ivorio, a wonderful brand of juice from the Ivory Coast- pineapple is the most common and the tastiest- and eat small roasted peanuts, fresh papaya, and if we're lucky and can find one at a corner vendor, palm sprouts. We roll along the surprisingly nice highway, slowing every few miles for a town. Tintinbougou, Zantaguila, Marka-couga, Fougani, Fana, Zambougou... Every town has a speed bump with an official looking person watching, sometimes talking to our driver, and then waving us on. Women hold up food and drink for our journey. Often a boy offers a live chicken, carrying it upside down by its feet.

Past the big city of Segou the road becomes rougher and we have to slow down. We pass through several tollbooths. After inspecting the truck's stickers, looking at the driver's registration and accepting about a dollar toll, the man lifts the gate and we continue on. We turn left at Bla and drive over a branch of the Niger, eventually making it to San just after dark.

The next morning, following a breakfast of bread, butter, jam and tea, we leave San behind, passing through more checkpoints. We drive by a shallow lake, stopping to give a coin and a blessing to a group of boys on the side of the road who were recently circumcised. We angle northeast as we pass Kong, Ouan, Baramandougou, Sokoura, Ganga, slowing to a crawl through some of the towns during their market day. We finally reach Sevare in Mopti district then turn back east to Bandiagara in Dogon country. In the not too distant past, the Dogon was the most visited area in Mali. With interesting people, cliff dwellings, massive ornate masks, and beautiful vistas, it is truly a remarkable area.

The road past Bandiagara is dirt as we descend into a huge valley, passing a large town called Bankass (really) and then about twenty miles later, we finally, mercifully, arrive in Koro.

Koro itself is just about what you imagine. A dusty town of maybe 30,000 people. It's telling that on the drive to Koro many larger cities have roundabouts in the center with a monument of some kind. The one in Bandiagara is especially impressive. Probably forty feet tall, it has huge cement replicas of the decorated wooden ladders that lean against nearly every hut holding up a gigantic dinner plate. The plate represents the pottery dating back over 11,000 years that has been found in the area around Bandiagara. This is arguably the oldest pottery in the world and put the town on the map for anthropologists. By contrast, arriving in Koro, in order to go left towards the school, one must first negotiate a roundabout composed of a pile of rocks, old tires and what looks like a beach ball in the center. Made up mainly of farmers and small business owners, the village is dry, secluded and very, very poor.

But this is home to the founder of Grace School, Ibrahima Kodio. He lives here with his wife Rachel, their three young girls, several pigs and chickens, a donkey, and up to ten students and relatives. In Mali, it's not an unusual arrangement to have fifteen people in a single house. The Kodios live in a rented dwelling constructed of mud bricks. The main house has four small rooms: three bedrooms and a family room. An adjacent building has just enough space for the boys to lie down at night. There is a single outhouse and no running water. Solar panels provide enough electricity to intermittently charge phones and power a television and a few lights.

In the morning, the older students head to the original Grace School location, just off the main street, in the rented space where it all started back in 2010. Rachel, her three daughters, and the younger students all walk to the new location. The first three classrooms opened in time for the 2015-16 school year. It holds grades one through four of the growing school. By spring of 2016, the second set of classrooms was being built.

With over a hundred students and at least twenty employees, with the construction jobs created, with the spiritual and philosophical shifts that the school has already caused in the town, Grace is by any measure a success. But it hasn't always been this way.

———————

Sangha is a remarkable village. Built on a high plateau overlooking the Gondo Plain, the views are breathtaking. Homes are constructed of locally quarried stone. Unlike in much of Mali, and even on the plains below, mud brick construction is rare. Without the dust and dirt the whole settlement has a clean look. The children's dark skin shines in a way that is unusual and stunning.

The French ethnologist Marcel Griaule made the town famous by using it as a base for his study of the Dogon people. His somewhat controversial and largely discredited 1948 book about Dogon traditions and beliefs, still in print today, brought new interest to the area, intriguing scientists and adventurers alike.

The first Protestant Christian influence in the area came through the Christian and Missionary Alliance (CMA). A former Presbyterian named A.B. Simpson founded the CMA in the 19th century. Simpson left his pastorate in his native Canada in 1873 to lead a church in Louisville, Kentucky. He then moved to New York to pastor the Thirteenth Street Presbyterian Church. His interest in providing aid and evangelizing to the flood of immigrants arriving in the city caused problems with church leadership and eventually led to his resignation. Simpson established the Gospel Tabernacle in the midst of the poorest of the poor and made it clear that all were invited. In time he came to the realization that his calling was to minister to the unreached masses, not only in New York, but around the world. A series of camp meetings and revivals eventually led to the founding of the CMA.

As the organization grew, the first missionaries were sent out to the Congo in 1884. The group continued to thrive even after Simpson's death in 1919, spreading throughout the world, including to outposts in West Africa.

In an apocryphal story related by Jeanne Smith, who was a missionary in the area for over thirty years, a Dogon went to Guinea looking for work in 1930. The CMA was ministering in Guinea by then, and soon after the man began attending services he accepted Christ. This put the Dogon area of Mali on CMA's radar and led to Reverend Frances James McKinney and his wife Laura's assignment there.

9

The McKinney's were understandably nervous about being transferred from the Congo to this unknown area. The Dogons were animists for the most part, worshiping idols and performing sacrifices. Goats and chickens were typically used as a blood offering but it was rumored that occasionally humans were used. They believed that if blood didn't seep into the ground, the harvest would be poor. There is a legend of a French commander located at Sangha that was told to stay in his house during a night of fetish celebrations. He couldn't resist the urge to go out and was never heard of again.

But the McKinney's arrived anyway, setting up a mission in the village on the edge of the plateau. Jeanne remembers the story of their first convert. A Dogon witch doctor named Asegerama went on a trip. While he was away a heavy rain destroyed the mud house where he kept the idols, or in Dogon, his *ammas*. When he returned and saw the mud covered idols he said, "You are my gods and you can't even take care of yourselves. How can I expect you to care for me? Where is the true Amma?"

That night Asegerama had a dream. He saw a white man standing under a tree with an open book in his hands. That white man said, "If you come to me I will tell you of Amma." Several days later he went to the weekly market at Sangha. As he was walking by a small field below the mission at Sangha he saw a white man standing under a tree holding an open book. He recognized him as the man from his dream. He went over to Frances (Mac) McKinney and said to him, "I saw you in my dream and you told me you would show me the way to Amma." Mac was surprised and thrilled. He explained the way to Amma through Christ and Asegerama became the first Christian in Dogon land. He took the McKinney's to his village, explaining to the people that he had been wrong and that this man would lead them to the true Amma. Then the message went to the next village along the escarpment and in that way spread quickly, creating many converts. The McKinney's did most of their early work on horseback. Mac got a Jeep later and was able to encourage the creation of roads, which made it possible to go down through the sand to Koro and Bono and elsewhere in the plains.

Jeanne Smith was eleven years old and at a church camp in California when she received her call to mission work in Africa. Five years later at the same camp, when she was alone in the chapel, she felt an unmistakable anointing to work in Mali. She met John McKinney in Florida during her last two years of high school. The son of Mac and Laura, he grew up among the Dogon and planned to return to Sangha as a missionary. It would be another three years, when they both ended up at Nyack Missionary College in New York, before they reconnected. They got married in 1962 in the year between their junior and senior years.

They studied French for a year in Paris and finally arrived in Mali in 1966 with their two children. Privately Jeanne and John had a difficult marriage from the start but they made great missionaries. She was the first to teach Sunday School there. She remembers that Dogons have always been interested in learning new things. There was a school in Sangha when they arrived and over the next several years six more were added in towns on the plains. School was conducted using the Dogon language.

Tom Burns was one of the early missionaries. He developed a Dogon language course for new arrivals from the US, as few of the local people could speak French. Interestingly, in order for Dogons to become pastors they had to go to Bible School in N'Torosso where the courses were taught in Bambara. Jeanne noticed right away that Dogons have an amazing aptitude for language. The fact that some learned Bambara, French, and even English helped with the unification of the districts.

Although much of the population was converted from their animist beliefs to Christianity, many Dogon still hold on to their ancient traditions. Divination plots in the sand in which fox tracks provide meaning, grain and animal sacrifices, and clay or carved idols are still common throughout the area. There are an estimated 30,000 Christian Dogons, most of whom follow the CMA tradition, although there are a number of Catholics as well. Of course there is a strong Muslim influence now. Ninety-five percent of Malians consider themselves Muslim, three percent are Christian, and about two percent follow animist religions.

The impressive stone church and many of the other buildings designed by the missionaries and built with the help of the local people remain in use today. They are owned and maintained by the Dogon Church. Jeanne and John Smith left Sangha in 1990 and no missionaries have been assigned there since. A huge celebration took place in the village in January 2012 when five thousand gathered to welcome CMA representatives who delivered the first Dogon translation of the bible.

Ibrahima recalls Jeanne and the others fondly. He remembers the church services and the excitement that everyone felt when the mangos from the big tree were ripe. The missionaries would collect them all into a storage shed and then have a big festival in which they were distributed to the local families. Families with more children would receive a larger share of the healthy fruit. The missionaries grew lettuce, tomatoes and other vegetables as well.

On the other hand, Marcel Griaule and the French brought the onions. Sangha is still known for their wonderful onions, the Dogon's only cash crop. They are shipped as far away as the Ivory Coast to use in onion sauce, a staple of many African diets. Griaule was instrumental in damming a small seasonal stream on the plateau. This provided enough water to grow onions along its banks. They are irrigated by hand much of the year, workers carrying bowls of water to sprinkle on the plants, or using hoses with simple pumps. It is still a striking scene to see lush, vibrant, green onion fields in the otherwise dry, red and brown landscape.

Below Sangha and extending for over twenty miles in each direction is the Bandiagara escarpment, a UNESCO World Heritage Site. The Dogon people have lived in and around the cliff face since at least the 15th century. The original inhabitants, the small and mysterious Tellem, built structures into the cliffs centuries earlier. Probably hunters, they vanished soon after the arrival of the Dogon.

The Dogon themselves, although more agriculturally based, didn't live on the plain until the early part of the 20th century. They cultivated small farms and then returned to the escarpment at night for safety. It was into this world that Ibrahima Kodio's parents were born. David in Ibi and Louise in Amani. While Louise's family was Christian, David's never converted. In 1974, soon after the two married, David became very sick with a respiratory illness. CMA missionaries paid to have him sent to their hospital in Ferkessedougou, Ivory Coast. When he returned to Ibi his family rejected him, as they felt that he had been healed by dark magic.

———————

So, following the birth of David and Louise's first daughter, named Nema, which means Grace in Dogon, and their first son, Zacharie, they moved to Sangha. David continued to receive treatment for his respiratory problems, which thankfully eventually resolved. Here they had Ibrahima in 1977, and were blessed with three more boys and another girl. Education was always important to the Kodios. They stressed it at home and encouraged the children to continue their studies. Ibrahima graduated from high school in Sevare and then moved to the capital to study physics. He received his degree from the University of Bamako in 2002. Zacharie became an engineer, Joseph an attorney and there are two nurses in the family as well. All are life long learners.

Ibrahima trained for three years as a mechanic for small aircraft in a program for aviation missionaries. His love of Jesus and his love for tinkering led him down this path that seemed perfect at the time. He would be able to fly into isolated areas of Mali and other countries to provide medical help and to teach the villagers about Jesus. When an opportunity arose to continue his training in Australia, he jumped at it. Excited about the prospect of improving his English and his mechanical skills, he had high hopes. Unfortunately, the program wasn't a good one. He effectively became a prisoner of the company. The students worked very hard for little pay. Ibrahima wore the same shirt for six months because he couldn't afford a new one. He had no free time, poor food, and no opportunity to explore his surroundings. For someone who loved to learn new things and to practice new languages and accents, learning the slang and clichés of a culture, he felt stifled and disappointed.

He dropped out of the program about the same time that the owners restructured it. This led to the lowest point in Ibrahima's life. Returning to Koro was one of the hardest things he could have done. When people move away, when they see Bamako, and especially when they have experienced life outside of Mali, it is very unusual to return home. Everyone thought that he was crazy, mentally unstable. He remembers people staying away from him during these years. His close friends didn't understand. He even began to wonder about his own sanity. If no one else would return to Koro, why did he?

Ibrahima began teaching physics at the public high school, a job that he could do in his sleep. He instinctively understood the subject and enjoyed teaching it.

His gift of language served him well as a guide for tourists and visitors to the area. The history of the region, the ancient beliefs, the old legends are as much a part of Ibrahima as the treacherous cliff paths that he still navigates with ease. It was as a guide that he met a group of health care workers from the States. Conversations with them led to periodic jobs working as a medical translator in clinics hundreds of miles away, south of Bamako.

It seems that most people in Mali wear many hats to make a living. In addition to being a Dogon guide, installing and servicing solar panels, teaching school, and training as an airplane mechanic, he also became a medical translator. A natural leader, he quickly became indispensible to the medical mission groups that he worked with. He helped organize transportation, lodging, and more translators for the teams. He arranged currency exchangers and found the best pizza in Bamako. His English continued to improve as he worked with people from the US more regularly. His knowledge of a multitude of Malian dialects grew as well.

As much as Ibrahima enjoyed all of his different jobs, he was disappointed that the flight mechanic career hadn't worked out. He still felt a strong pull to spread the Gospel and didn't have an opportunity to do so. He could talk about Christ to the US missionaries of course, and to other people that he came into contact with, but he didn't feel it was enough. Speaking about religion at the public school where he spent the majority of his time was discouraged.

In 2004 he heard about a beautiful, intelligent, faith filled woman living in Sevare named Rachel. Her story was compelling and he knew he had to meet her. They became inseparable and soon fell in love. They married in his parent's tiny farming village near the escarpment on December 27, 2009.

Grace Private School began as a vision and a prayer in the fall of 2009. It was the two most important things in Ibrahima's life- education and faith- rolled into one. Like public schools throughout Mali, the ones in dusty, remote Koro were overcrowded and underfunded.

In Mali the Ministry of Education governs the education system. There are nine grades in what is called the Fundamental Education, divided into two cycles. Grades one through six are the first cycle. In the sixth grade, all students take the primary school completion exam (CEP) that allows them to enter the second cycle, which is grades seven through nine. All instruction is given in French, the national language, which usually isn't spoken at home except in the wealthiest families. English instruction typically begins in the seventh grade.

At the end of ninth grade the students sit for the Diplome d'Études Fondamentales (DEF), which is necessary in order to advance to high school. The pass rate of this test is only around 15%. To make matters worse, passing the test is no guarantee of admission to high school. Although the government really ramped up primary school attendance about fifteen years ago, secondary school has not kept up. There simply aren't enough schools or teachers to meet the demand.

Kit's important to keep in mind that Mali has one of the fastest growing populations in the world. A nearly 3% annual growth rate means that 450,000 people are added to the population of 15 million *every single year.* And once again, it is the rural girls who suffer. They end up having the poorest rate of graduation from both middle school and high school.

School is free and compulsory for all children between the ages of seven and sixteen, although many still do not attend for various reasons. Some are needed to help at home and on the

16

farm. For others, even the uniforms and school supplies are too expensive. In a country with an average annual income of less than a thousand dollars, there isn't money for extras. In 2007 only 68% of boys and 54% of girls ages seven to twelve were enrolled in school. The CIA World factbook website reports that an abysmal 48% of men and 29% of women over the age of fifteen can read and write.

Because education was so important to Ibrahima and his family growing up, he always felt called to be a teacher. Whether formally, as in his public high school physics position, or informally, by showing younger people how to repair a motorcycle or to install a solar panel, he was always teaching or learning.

So, when the idea to start a school came to him, it felt natural. It also felt terrifying. He literally had no money. And no way to raise any. All he had was a dream and a drive that comes from inside, and he knew that he at least try had to try. A school would help improve the opportunities for children in Koro and he would be able to teach them about God in a free and open manner.

That first school year he had only seventeen students scattered among grades seven to nine. They fit easily in the rented building on the main road through town. Rachel became the administrator and Ibrahima taught, as did a total of thirteen part time teachers. He also continued to teach full time at the public high school.

Funds for the school came mainly from the small amount of money he was able to save by translating for medical missionaries from the US. He was helping several weeks a year with groups from Utah and Kansas City. Even the modest amount that he made those weeks was more than he earned in a year of teaching.

He did charge tuition, but many families could not pay. From the beginning, Ibrahima was more interested in educating children and teaching the Gospel than in balancing the books. He collected what he could and supplemented with money from his own pocket to pay for rent, salaries, and school supplies.

That first year required a tremendous amount of faith and prayer. His first daughter, Catherine, was born that autumn and the young family stretched their limited resources to the limit.

With prayer and simplicity, everyone not only survived, but thrived. The children and their parents liked the small classes and extra attention. They worked hard, and in the end it paid off. Of the seven students in ninth grade, six of them passed the DEF. It was an incredible success and a validation that Ibrahima was right where he needed to be.

Never one to sit still or to have only one job when he could have four, he continued to translate for the medical missionaries several times a year. He also kept his full time job at the public high school and maintained several solar panels for businesses around Mali. All of this work brought in just enough money to pay rent on his own house and the school and to provide simple meals for his family.

By the start of the 2011/2012 school year the number of enrolled students had grown. More than sixty children across the three grade levels now filled the small rented space. This required more teachers and a larger budget. A few parents paid tuition faithfully but most did not. The Kodios were housing several children in their own home and they were still subsidizing the budget with every spare CFA that they could find. Ibrahima knew that the situation wasn't sustainable long term, but he worked from the heart and the spirit rather than the mind when it came to the children. He felt that if this was where God wanted him to be, the path would one day become clear.

Chapter 2
A Dream Fulfilled as New Dreams Arise

It was an email for which I had been waiting for years. Most of those without even knowing it. Following my somewhat mystical call back to God in 2004 I knew that I wanted to help others in some way. Certainly I became a better, more compassionate doctor, but I felt that there was more that I could do. In 2008 I met Eric and Jodi Garbison from Cherith Brook Catholic Worker and began cleaning restrooms there on my days off. Getting to know the homeless, addicted, mentally ill, and discarded while scrubbing down the showers was a step in the right direction. I knew by then that the way to Jesus was down. The kingdom of God is found on the opposite end of prestige, titles, wealth, comfort, pride, and security.

Around the same time, I found a new church and a wonderful pastor. Holly McKissick shared my vision of justice and reconciliation. Ex-prisoner or recent immigrant, urban hipster or suburban family, the congregation was inclusive and diverse. Meeting other people on the same path, attending services, teaching Sunday School classes and reading my Bible every day allowed God to continue to work in my heart.

It was on a drive to and from Wichita in the fall of 2011 that I spoke it out loud for the first time. Sister Therese Bangert and I were on the board of the Kansas Coalition Against the Death Penalty together and she had asked to ride with me to the annual meeting. I was thrilled to have her company and she was an outstanding travel companion. She asked questions and listened as the miles rolled by.

I remember driving through the subtle beauty of the Flint Hills on the return trip when the subject of mission work came up. I told her that I hadn't found the right fit. The ones through church involved building things. Two years prior I had undergone shoulder surgery, so I was nervous about heavy lifting. What I really wanted was to find something medical. I really only felt comfortable when I was working or at home, so it just seemed ideal to do a mission that felt like my job as much as possible.

I had been looking around and nothing seemed to fit. As a urologist, my skills were fairly specialized. Most places called for a wider scope of practice of medicine, like what is found in a general surgeon or an emergency room physician. Many required a longer commitment then I had available. Sister Therese listened compassionately and pragmatically. She said she would pray that I would find my place. She is an incredible person, an outspoken and effective advocate for children and prisoners, and I felt relief just knowing that she was in my corner.

The email came not more than two weeks later. One of my partners forwarded an appeal from a local group named Medical Missions Foundation (MMF). They were looking for a urologist to fill a spot on an upcoming trip. There was a twelve-year-old girl that required a urologic operation. It was so improbable, so providential, that I felt like the note was directed right at me. I knew that I had to do it. The fact that we would be going to Mali, a country that I was pretty sure that I had never heard of, didn't faze me.

After finding out more information and learning we would be leaving in less than six weeks, some anxiety hit. And yet I kept moving forward. Yellow fever shot, visa application, call schedule adjustment, and several spray bottles of permethrin later I was ready to go. My family was as supportive as one would expect under the circumstances. My first long trip away from home was to an impoverished country in West Africa. The unknowns weighed on them, but neither Lucie nor the kids suggested I shouldn't do it.

When the forty-two of us arrived in Mali it was nearly midnight. I had read all of the information that I could about the country but had kept to myself for the most part on the journey. So, I really didn't know what to expect.

As we made our way through customs and to the hectic, crowded, hot baggage claim area I met Ibrahima. Later he said that he knew it was me right away. He knew a urologist was coming and in the group of new faces he picked mine out as the one.

The week was difficult and amazing. We worked long hours. Nothing went the way that I had planned and yet everything was perfect. The operating table was on cinder blocks. Stirrups were created from coat racks. We improvised and made do. It was my first important lesson in African ingenuity. I was able to help the young girl. When she recovered she would be normal and not leak urine anymore. She would be able to go back to school.

Although we were very busy I still had time to feel homesick. There was no wifi and my cellphone didn't work for international calls, so I wasn't able to call Jackson on his tenth birthday. Two days later, knowing how much I missed my family, anesthesiologist Lisa Heath said I could borrow her phone to call

Sofia on her twelfth birthday. Excited about the possibility, I needed to wait until I knew she would be home from school and ballet practice.

We finished our surgeries by about eight in the evening, but another room was still going. So I sat outside under the stars waiting to use Lisa's phone. I had met Ibrahima but hadn't really talked to him at that point. He was in charge of the translators and much else and wasn't around most of the time. But that night he sat with me while I waited.

We talked about the US, about God, about his church and mine, about our families and our hopes and dreams. I found that allowing for differences in culture and socioeconomic status we were very similar. We both felt called to help others and to work for reconciliation and peace. We both knew the importance of education, especially for girls. It was an amazing discussion.

He also let me know that his father had been suffering from urinary problems. He had been praying for help. When he found out that a urologist was coming to the clinic at Ouelessebougou for the first time he felt that his prayers had been answered. Ibrahima explained the symptoms. He was beyond grateful to learn that in fact I did have a medication that would likely help him. He would deliver it to his father over five hundred miles away when he returned home.

Eventually I was able to talk to my kids and wish them happy birthday, which completed the extraordinary night. From that time on I felt more at ease, the rest of the week going by in a rush. I did visit with Ibrahima a few more times that trip and he presented me with a Dogon door. It was a small reproduction of a beautifully intricate story-telling door that was once common in his area of the country.

When I returned to the States and tried to go back to work it seemed that everything had changed. The quiet streets, the solitary lives, the accumulation of things that fill our oversized houses, seemed foreign. Like many before me who had made the transition back to the reality of our lives in the land of plenty, I struggled against it. I didn't want to lose the awakening that had begun in Mali.

I wrote and thought and prayed and in time two things happened. A spot opened up on the Uganda trip in the fall, which I quickly grabbed. And I decided to bring Ibrahima to the US.

His visit wasn't planned out in detail. I simply knew that I wanted to show him my world. Like everyone, Ibrahima's understanding of God was filtered by what he has seen. In his case it had been through the CMA missionaries and the Dogon Church, through the YouTube end times prophesy videos that he watched for hours when he had Internet access, and through the Mormon missionaries that had helped him in recent years. The only Westerners that he had met were those that were there to care for the poorest of the poor, or that were on vacation through the Bandiagara escarpment. Either way it was a very skewed sample of unusual people that spent their money and their vacation time to fly halfway around the world to a place that few others would venture.

As the lead translator for two or three yearly missions over the previous five years, as a guide in his part of the country, he had met hundreds of people from the US. And yet I could tell that he still didn't understand. He didn't understand why we did it. Care for himself, his family, his village and his tribe, yes. But why care for someone so far away, so foreign? We were all rich in his eyes. Why do we share with someone so far away?

In our time in Mali we had talked about poverty in the States, something that he couldn't understand. We have so much – how can there possibly be poverty? We talked about homelessness and mental illness, about soup kitchens and food pantries. He had been fascinated with this but simply couldn't picture it.

I felt called to show him. To show him as much of the variety of life in the United States as I could. To show him my church and to let him visit the churches of his other US friends. To show him poverty and need in a land of plenty and to talk together about why it exists. To show him the empty sidewalks of our neighborhoods and how we isolate ourselves in our cars and homes. That we spend our lives much more alone. And to show him that really, we are all the same. That regardless of nationality, religion, and income level, we are all created by and loved by God. We all have the same needs and dreams.

I discovered that Ibrahima had several friends that were interested in helping host him during his visit. I had very peripherally known an amazing couple named Josh and Josie Uecker. Friends of my sister, they had both been to Mali as certified registered nurse anesthetists. They had also become friends with Ibrahima and were thrilled to hear that he was coming to visit. We had begun planning for his visit earlier that summer. Christina Corvino (then Eldridge) had been the mission coordinator for the Mali trip in 2012 and she was happy to be involved. Local musician Barclay Martin was on board as well. We all met prior to Ibrahima's arrival and did some preliminary planning.

A letter to the US embassy in Mali, multiple emails and a plane ticket later, Ibrahima arrived in Kansas City in August 2012 for a five-week visit. To see our culture through his eyes that first week is something I won't ever forget. Those weeks were a blessing for all that encountered him. I learned that a big smile and a sincere, "How are you?" can open many doors.

He had lived in Australia a few years prior but hadn't been able to see very much of it. He had no money there and no friends to show him around. So to experience the gigantic, clean, open aisles of Target or Trader Joe or Hy-Vee for the first time was a revelation. All of the choices were overwhelming. In rural

Mali there were no choices. Dinner was usually one dish and there was not much variety.

In Mali there was very little money for anything except the absolute necessities. There are no knickknacks in the house, no bookshelves, no books, no pantries, no pictures on the wall, no decorative lamps or soft carpet, no granite cabinet tops, no kitchens for that matter, no three car garages, no cars. We spent a lot of time just walking up and down aisles looking at things. Watching people load up their carts with toys, electronics, food, toiletries, clothes, greeting cards, drinks, and bags of candy with Ibrahima was like seeing it all for the first time.

He stayed with my family for the first week. We were able to spend time talking. I learned much more about life in Mali. And for the first time I learned about Grace School.

It had been in existence for two years by that point. He had been funding it with his own money and with tuition from the few families that actually paid it. He was excited but very anxious about the future. Of his thirty-six ninth graders, thirty-three had passed the DEF exam to be eligible to enter high school. It was an unbelievable number. The plan was to add first grade but as poor as the area was, he didn't know if the school was going to be sustainable.

Public schools are free in theory but in fact do have a price. Parents are expected to buy a few school supplies and often a uniform. Simply having the children in class and not helping with chores at home and on the farm has a cost as well.

The public schools are very crowded. Classes often have sixty children in them. Students don't have their own books. The few texts are for classroom use only. Teachers are typically poorly trained. Advanced degrees aren't required. In fact, nearly anyone with a modest education can become a teacher. In a country of such tremendous unemployment, any steady job is in high demand even if it pays poorly. The fact that Ibrahima has a degree in advanced physics and teaches that subject at the high school level is unusual in a remote town like Koro.

So, for parents that want their children to have a better education, maybe to have a chance to do something beyond farming with their lives, a school like Grace is enticing. And as we've seen, the area has a fair number of Christian families that would love their children to have Bible classes as well. To be able to grow up in community with other believers.

To learn about this for the first time through Ibrahima was eye-opening. It truly felt like God had a hand in bringing us together. I knew that we could do better. That my new friends and I could help alleviate much of his financial concern. I knew that if there is one thing people in the US are good at, it's supporting causes like this.

During his stay I was in conversation with Christina and Josie, telling them what I was discovering about Grace. We arranged to have him visit local schools to see examples of how things are done in both public and private settings.

He gave talks at several churches in the area. To his surprise he began raising money. When he told them about Grace School people immediately wanted to help. His circle of friends widened.

Although he wasn't able to visit them, Ibrahima was in contact with the group of medical missionaries from Utah as well. They had been good friends over the years and were instrumental in getting him his first medical translating job. Simply having access to high speed Internet during those weeks was immensely helpful in rekindling some old friendships.

About halfway through his time in the US, Ibrahima was introduced to Dennis and Judy Uecker. Josh's father Dennis is the co-pastor and business administrator of a local church, a retired salesperson and real estate agent. Judy is a wonderful mom and does administrative tasks at their church. Although they have never been to Africa nor are health care workers or educators, they are passionate Christians. They were mesmerized by Ibrahima's message. His humility, simplicity, and zeal for the Lord really spoke to them in an unexpected and profound way.

Judy remembers, "We made a trip to Iowa to stay with Steve & Lois Smith, Josie's parents, and to visit their church. That trip stands out to me because Ibrahima talked to two different groups while there, one adult and one teen, and he was able to just be himself, share about Grace School, and connect with these groups so easily. It seems that wherever we went and whomever he talked with, whether planned or not, Christian or not, his love for them shined through and he impacted people."

My first medical mission to Uganda coincided with the last portion of Ibrahima's visit. Consequently I didn't meet Dennis and Judy until after he had returned to Mali. Once I was back in the US and was able to focus on life in the land of plenty again, I met with both sets of Ueckers. We reflected on our experience with Ibrahima. We talked about what we had learned and what we could have done differently.

In the end Ibrahima returned to Mali with $4500 to put towards the school's expenses. Humble and gracious, he hadn't expected to raise any money at all, but people couldn't resist his story. This amount was nearly three times the previous year's budget. It would pay rent and salaries, but more importantly it brought security and comfort that the 2012/2013 school year would be a success.

As a group, the five of us felt like we could provide more than a one-time gift. From that meeting we formed Grace Missions Inc. The nonprofit, 501(c)3 corporation's initial goal was to support Grace Private School on an ongoing business. We put together an email list from the contacts we had accumulated over the prior few months. Dennis filed the government forms and agreed to keep the books. Judy started an email newsletter using Ibrahima's updates and Josie created a Facebook page. I wrote an occasional blog, and Josh, our president, kept us all in line. It was then, and still remains, a very simple endeavor with a very simple mission.

Soon after my first visit to Mali the already tenuous government fell apart. A military coup took place on March 21, 2012, ending President Amadou Toure's ten-year reign just prior to the April presidential elections. The coup was in part due to controversy surrounding longstanding issues with the Tuaregs in the northeast part of the country. The instability created an opportunity for Tuareg rebels to take over several towns, once again calling for an independent state.

Civilian interim President Dioncounda Traore was beaten unconscious in May but he held onto power. A group of Islam extremists, Ansar Dine, in addition to a Tuareg group, began destroying Muslim shrines and artifacts in Timbuktu, Gao, and Kidal. By autumn they had consolidated control in those areas and had begun moving closer to the more populated southwest part of the country. Around the same time, a consortium of African nations in cooperation with France announced that they were planning military action for sometime after the first of the year.

With travel warnings and at least some threat of violence towards foreigners, the official MMF trip planned for January 2013 was cancelled. A few of us had been closely monitoring the situation. We waited until the Uganda trip was complete before talking seriously about returning to Mali. Surgeon Tammy Neblock and mission coordinator Abigail Hayo had been there several times before and were comfortable with the risks. I felt like I really needed to get back there- to help medically and to talk to Ibrahima about Grace School. Communication with Mali was extremely difficult. Koro had inadequate cellular service and terrible Internet access. Face to face meetings were really the only way to catch up.

So the three of us, plus Pepper Card, an operating room nurse who also was a veteran of many missions, traveled to Mali in January. We had read about refugee camps in Burkina Faso where moderate Tuaregs and others had fled with their animals and a few belongings. Many had been there for a year and we knew they would feel hopeless and homesick. It was very difficult to obtain information on the camps from the US. The plan was to bring medicine and see if we could screen and treat patients on site.

We brought Dr. Oumar Bagayoko, the physician who runs the private clinic in Ouelessebougou where we work in Mali. A follower of Islam, he is one of the holiest people that I know. We also brought Yeah Samake, the mayor and historically one of our advocates in Mali. Ibrahima also came with us, in addition to Korotimi Haidara, a wonderful translator and friend. So the four Westerners and the four Malians attempted for two days to be granted access to the refugees. We were able to talk briefly with them several times at the camps, but never could provide medical care. The number of officials, police and political figures that we met with and that wanted to meet with us kept multiplying to the point that we knew it was hopeless. We drove twelve hours back across Burkina to the capital and flew home to Bamako. It was a memorable trip and important for several reasons. The refugees were so happy that we had come to see them. To have people from the US travel all that way touched them deeply. And to be able to speak to people from their own country...they were beyond words. They said that we were the first visitors they had had apart from the NGO's that ran the camps.

We returned to Ouelessebougou and had a busy forty-eight hours of surgery and medical visits in Dr. Oumar's clinic. Everyone benefitted immensely from the partnership with his clinic. We provided medications, continuing education, and validation for all of the hard work that he put into his career. We, in turn, were infinitely blessed to be able to care for the poor rural Malians and to take part in such a rewarding cultural exchange.

I was able to catch up with Ibrahima that week. He had stories, pictures and anecdotes of Grace School for me. It was a frightening, unstable time. The French military began their attack on the extremists while we were there. The fighting wasn't very close to where we were, but it wasn't too far north of Koro. Ibrahima later found that he had friends and relatives that were affected, forced to flee, even killed. I could see the concern on his face as we listened to radio reports of the conflict.

It was the first of several years of uncertainty in the Dogon. Some parents used the political situation as an excuse to keep their children home from school. Others left the area completely. There were intermittent skirmishes and unpredictable violent attacks on Christians and moderate Muslims. Koro itself was thankfully spared.

Upon returning to Kansas City I met with the others to let them know what I had discovered. Grace School was doing much better with the cash infusion. One hurdle that we needed to overcome was how to get funds to Ibrahima on an ongoing basis. He had carried cash with him from the US and I had brought him another thousand dollars. But it would likely be another year before I saw him again and he was going to need more money.

In between his other duties he did eventually find a bank that felt safe. It took him nearly two months to get to Sevare and open an account. I knew from my trips to Africa that everything moves slowly and feels extremely complicated. And many times the way that we initially want things done turns out to not be feasible, nor even the best option.

Money is treated differently in Mali. People spend what they have on their immediate needs. And if they have more than what is needed for rent and food, their friends and family often learn about it and ask for handouts. Community is many times stronger in Mali, and without a second thought people share what they have. This isn't limited to Christians of course. One of the tenets of Islam is the Zakas, which means purifying one's wealth for the will of Allah. Tithing and sharing freely are deeply ingrained.

Consequently, we found that it made Ibrahima nervous to have a large amount of money with no immediate need. He knew that word would leak out and it would cause trouble with his family and friends. He would feel obligated to share.

It's unusual for people to have bank accounts. Extra money is more typically put into land or animals. Or another wife. Although not tolerated among the small Christian Malian population, it is very common for Malian men to have more than one wife. Once one family is well cared for, extra income or a windfall profit is a temptation to start another one.

Following further research and intermittent discussions, Dennis determined the least expensive method to wire money to Ibrahima's bank. For just a few dollars we were able to get him cash when he needed it. With very limited funds in the Grace Missions account we sent it only when he asked. We found Ibrahima to be a meticulous record keeper, providing detailed monthly reports listing expenditures to the nearest CFA. With the CFA's value at about two tenths of a US cent each, we felt very comfortable that we knew where the money was going.

By April, the French government began removing their troops as the violence had lessened in the north. The children at Grace School finished up their year in Koro. One of the things that Ibrahima did from the beginning was have a big party in late May called Student's Day. There was singing, music, movies, dancing and praying. Videos of the event show presentations by the teachers, students in special new t-shirts, dance contests and a huge amount of food. It's something that everyone looks forward to all year and is a great morale builder.

The final event of the school year is the DEF exam for the ninth graders. In June 2013 there were thirty-four students that took the DEF. Knowing how important the test is to their future, the teachers and students take it very seriously. They study, prepare and pray. Both the children raised Christian and those raised Muslim pray together every day, and test day is no different. Ibrahima said there was a rumor that there was some kind of witchcraft taking place over at Grace School. People saw them praying to Jesus in a group, something that's an unusual sight in that area. It all paid off as once again the pass rate was well above the national average. Twenty-six students passed for an average of 76%. It was another successful year and a source of great pride for Ibrahima, Rachel, the teachers, and all of his many supporters.

Ibrahima at the Dogon (CMA) Church in Sangha

Onion farms in Sangha

Traditional Dogon masks and costumes

Cliff dwellings in the Bandiagara Escarpment

The remnant of the Kodio home in Sangha.

Adults from left to right: Zacharie, Suzanne, Louise, Ibrahima, Daniel, Moses. At the home of Daniel and Louise Kodio.

Simple grass walled classrooms

Students in the inaugural year of Grace School.

Grace School students in the 2011/2012 year.

Second graders in their lean-to classroom.

Dr. Oumar Bagayoko's clinic in Ouelessebougou.

Pepper, Korotimi, Abigail, and Tammy at the Malian refugee
camp in Burkina Faso 2013.

2015 medical team in Ouelessebougou.

Abigail, Sophie, Korotimi, and Tammy

Students standing on the perimeter of the new school land.

Ibrahima and Rachel Kodio's home.

The new Grace School building.

Grace students conferring with each other.

Clean, filtered water after morning exercises.

Josie and Josh Uecker, Brandon Pomeroy, Judy and Dennis
Uecker

Brandon with some of the middle school students, Jan 2016.

Grace students, spring 2016.

Ibrahima and Rachel Kodio, with Louise, Ruth, and Catherine.

Chapter 3
Faith and Growth Among Chaos

As if Ibrahima Kodio didn't have enough going on in his life, he decided to help build a church. The congregation in Koro had outgrown its current building several years prior. Hundreds of people were left outside the Evangelical Christian Church, listening to services at the doors. In the US we are used to getting in and out of church in an hour. Services in Koro at times may go one for three hours or more. Leaving perhaps half of the worshipers outside in the heat or rain wasn't ideal.

Ibrahima explained to me that anyone who has gone away and come back is considered an expert. Especially someone who has friends from the US. Not just an expert on what they learned while away, but on anything and everything. He had been to Australia, to university, and now to the States, so he was called upon for opinions and consultations constantly.

There is likely some truth to that notion, but just as important is the fact that he was well respected in his community. He had a reputation for getting things done and that's what the church board was looking for in this project. He was given leadership over the committee to begin building a church that could hold over a thousand people.

When Ibrahima showed me the beautiful stone church in Sangha, he said it had given him a false sense of what the buildings should look like. Growing up in a tiny village, he assumed that bigger cities would have bigger churches. He was wrong. In this Muslim country with only small pockets of Christians, many of the building were tiny. In Sevare, in Bandiagara, even in Bamako, the meeting places he attended were tiny and made of mud bricks and thatched roofs.

The building that he envisioned for Koro would pay homage to the one in Sangha. His church was a descendant of that CMA church so it only seemed fitting that the buildings would have some similarities. Sanctuaries that he had visited in the US and had seen on television also had influenced him. It would be large enough to hold everyone.

Ibrahima took on the challenge, writing in July 2013, "For the church building project, I already face opposition but with the help of the Lord God we all serve, there is understanding. In fact when they appointed me to administrate the work, I looked carefully on the plan and found that there are thirteen pillars in it and it has no symmetry at all. It has three little doors for a thousand people. The elevation at the front was very little so that the people at the back would fight with their neck to see the preacher. And the offices in the building prevent some people to see each other in the congregation. The previous administrator of the project could not read plans and none in the team could do so. I thought we need to delete those pillars and have a symmetric building where everyone can easily see everyone in the building with enough doors. There was a lot of opposition to me because the plan was made and validated in 2009 and the budget was set according to the plan. After many meetings they agree with changing the plan. The engineer is working on it. And we hope he will produce a better plan this time, even though it may change a bit the cost of the building."

Ibrahima spent the summer getting that project off the ground and preparing for the upcoming school year. A Catholic school in Koro expanded in 2013, adding eight more classrooms. Students from kindergarten through middle school attended. It quickly became overcrowded and understaffed. The Malian government subsidizes 80% of Catholic school tuition. So the Koro school received 125,000 CFA (about 208 USD) annually per student- 100,000 from the government and 25,000 from tuition.

This created another challenge for Grace School, which charged 81,000 CFA tuition and received no government subsidy. Although Ibrahima and the rest of us felt like we were offering a superior product, it seemed like a fairly steep upward climb to enroll more students. Despite the fact that many families didn't pay and Grace Missions was helping cover these costs, we knew we needed to drop tuition.

It was a balance between giving families an opportunity to be involved with their children's education by having them pay something, and keeping tuition low enough to prevent them from being scared off. So we dropped tuition to 63,000 CFA for 9th grade, and less for the lower grades.

The goal was to have thirty children in each class. The public and Catholic schools averaged sixty which was clearly too many for one teacher to control. By fall 2013, Grace School had fourteen in the 9th grade, twenty-one in 8th and six in 7th. There were nine in 1st grade and eleven in 2nd. This was the first year that 2nd grade had been offered, as each year an additional grade was added.

The teachers were all very committed to the school and agreed to a pay cut of one thousand CFA per year. The lean times continued but Malians were used to them and took it in stride. They were happy to have a job, especially in light of continued conflict in the area.

Presidential elections had taken place in July, with Ibrahim Boubacar Keita winning decisively. The separatists in the north weren't pleased with his choice for Prime Minister, causing occasional isolated clashes. But the overall threat of violence had lessened, and by the fall of 2013 France had withdrawn 60% of its remaining troops from the area.

Although it wouldn't be an official MMF mission we did start planning a return to Mali, but my dream of traveling to Koro would have to wait. We didn't have enough time and the trip would still have been too dangerous.

In January 2014, ten people flew into Bamako. We spent the first part of the week in Dagabo village where Tammy, Abigail and Sophie had cultivated a deep relationship over the prior five years. They had started a successful village school and a nonprofit to help support it. Sleeping in huts and sharing in the hospitality of the very poor yet gracious people is a joy that is difficult to explain. There is a sense of community and contentment. They are truly living season to season but there is peace.

Next we drove from Dagabo to Dr. Oumar's clinic to see patients, distribute medications and perform surgery. Ibrahima, Korotimi and several others were there to help with translation. Because we weren't able to bring a large group, and really only had two surgeons, one nurse and an anesthetist, we didn't stay for five days like a full team would have. We worked very hard for three days and nights. There were so many stories in that short, intense period of time.

On one of the days a woman of about twenty, so pretty, very thin, dressed all in black with an endearing overbite entered the exam room. She spoke in Bambara for probably three minutes with a high-pitched nervous rapid voice. Ibrahima and Malian urologist, Dr. Diarra, listened silently while I watched and waited. Finally she grew quiet. Ibrahima looked concerned and hesitated before turning to me and saying, "Oh, this is a very bad story."

She had malaria and had been very sick for a long time. With no money to see a doctor, she had sought help from a woman who was a traditional healer. She said that she was taken somewhere away from her home and witchcraft was used. She was given different herbs and potions as she had expected, but then she was tied down and a surgical procedure was performed. There was no anesthesia, just pain, confusion and fear. She explained it all in graphic detail. The healer told her afterwards that she would never have children, would never have a husband.

Now she was alone in Ouelessebougou, far away from home. A small fruit stand in the market was her only source of income, making just enough to keep from starving. She was so sad, depressed and anxious. Ibrahima was shaken by the story. I wasn't sure what to think but felt that I might be able to help. After asking some questions I learned that her systems all functioned normally. A physical examination confirmed my suspicion. Like over 90% of Malian women, she had undergone a disfiguring and painful procedure called female circumcision. The practice is ingrained in the culture and is very difficult to change. This was what she remembered. As inhumane as it is however, her fears of not being able to have children or becoming a wife were unfounded.

With Ibrahima's translation and Dr. Diarra's medical help, we sat with her and explained that everything was fine. That she was a healthy beautiful woman who could do anything she wanted. That there was no reason that she couldn't marry and have children. We gave her some time to let it sink in, ignoring for a few minutes the crush of people waiting outside the door. We gave her the malaria medications, some vitamins and, hopefully, a fresh start to her life. She seemed to relax. Her nervous smile felt more genuine. I pray that we helped her, gave her some confidence, a little peace, and let her feel that she is worthy and not completely alone.

We returned to Bamako to relax for a day before the long slog back to the States. Ibrahima and I were able to spend a morning together catching each other up on the prior year. Grace School was going well. We talked about several students in particular. Although every single child is special and has struggled in ways that we can't fully comprehend, one story was particularly touching.

Mohamed Traoré, a twelve-year-old boy with the interesting nickname Vieux, had recently joined the Kodio household. His father had died in the dangerous gold mine in Sikasso District when Vieux was nine. For the previous three years his mother Rebecca, Rachel's cousin, had worked extremely hard trying to provide for her family by running a small laundry service.

That fall, Rebecca had passed away following a sudden illness at the CMA Hospital in Koutiala, Sikasso's capital. Vieux's story made it back to the Kodios who had a family meeting. They were so saddened and troubled by his situation that they agreed to let the orphan travel to Koro to live with them. Ibrahima wanted to be sure that he had a sense of family and a good education as he grew up. He said that Vieux was a joy to have around. He seemed happy and was the third noisiest person in the household of fifteen behind Ibrahima and his daughter Catherine.

Ibrahima had recently been spending time looking at land in and around Koro. He had two projects in mind. He wanted to find a spot for a high school. This could be a little bit outside of town, where the land was cheaper and there was more room. A more immediate need was for a new primary school site.

There was no room to expand on the small rented site where the school was at the time. The owner was a devout Muslim and although he was happy to have the rent money he wasn't very cooperative. There were only three classrooms, so the first and second grades had classes in a temporary structure made with grass walls. The extreme heat and dust made teaching and learning difficult.

He had his eye on a property about three blocks away from the current school. It wasn't very large but he felt that it would do. There was enough land to build a three-story structure to hold nine classrooms, with room for a small administrative building as well. The owner wasn't ready to sell but Ibrahima planted a seed in his mind that he was interested in buying it.

Purchasing property is the same in Mali as it is anywhere. There is a kind of game that's played between the owner and the buyer. As we've seen, Malians aren't typically interested in amassing large amounts of money in the bank. Extra funds are usually used to purchase land, animals, or additional wives. So, if a landowner isn't in need of any of those things he isn't likely to sell. I encouraged Ibrahima to keep working on the owner and also to keep looking around for alternative building sites.

We also talked about the new school itself. He had rough blueprints and a budget by then. The less expensive option would be to build all nine classrooms on one level. Mud bricks could be used and it could be built very quickly. However, that option would require more land than we would reasonably have access to, and the buildings wouldn't last very long.

The alternative was to build a very sturdy concrete frame building one story at a time. Three stories of three classrooms each. The first three classrooms would cost about sixty thousand USD. This included preparing the site and adding pit toilets and possibly an administrative building.

This was a much higher number than we had dealt with yet at Grace Missions. The monthly budget at the time was only about fifteen hundred dollars. We had been covering that but not with a lot of money to spare. I knew that he had raised nearly five thousand during his 2012 visit to the US, but sixty thousand?

After catching my breath, stalling a little as my mind and heart caught up a little, we discussed it more. We talked about the school's needs and our goals. Finally, I told Ibrahima that we would do it. That we would raise that amount of money, and that he would be able to start building by the spring of 2015. Now we just had to figure out how to make it happen.

Upon returning to the States, I met with the other members of Grace Missions to fill them in on what I had leaned. I showed them the pictures that Ibrahima had given me. The photos showed the land that he hoped to buy and the current school, including the grass walled classrooms.

As expected, the Ueckers were excited about the possibility of our own school building. We began talking about a big fundraiser. None of us had ever tried to raise that kind of money, but if that was what was needed, we were sure going to try.

Over the next few months, my sister Alison Janssen designed a beautiful logo for Grace Missions, and we had preliminary talks with people that might be willing to help. Melissa and Ben Neis stepped in that spring. Melissa agreed to head up the event planning and was instrumental in the success of the night.

She and Josie went door to door to small businesses all over town asking for donations. They worked to find corporate sponsors and they gathered items to auction. It was a huge amount of work and they did an amazing job.

Over the summer we worked on getting Ibrahima's visa approved. We also began work on the schedule for his weeks in the States. His circle of friends had grown from the visit two years earlier and we wanted to be sure that he had a chance to see everyone.

Local artist Shane Evans created a design for a t-shirt, Eli Chamberlain and Alex Holsinger agreed to play music, and many businesses and volunteers pitched in to help with food and drinks as the event neared.

There is always at least some sad news from Mali. In his May 2014 update Ibrahima reported that the mother of one of the 9th grade students passed away. With a life expectancy in the mid-fifties, death is never far away, and yet it is no less traumatic.

Ibrahima said at the time, "At three thirty in the morning my friend Korka Sagara knocked on my door asking me to join those who are to go dig the grave. When I was able to see clearly, I was so surprised by the large number of new graves. Most of them were graves of babies and children. I made sure that others had the same observation as me. To my question, a sad answer was given: so many kids are dying from malaria and typhoid; the graves by the hospital have even more children than this one. There seem to be so many sad things happening in this little town. Yet, we understand how God has protected and is protecting us in a place where fatal danger is ubiquitously permanent."

The students at Grace School finished the year with another miracle. Of the thirteen 9th grade students, an unbelievable twelve passed the DEF exam. It was a cause for celebration. The Student's Day party was another success. It showcased the talent and hard work of the children while providing them a well-earned reward. Despite setbacks, the constant threat of violence and a prolonged drought, the students and teachers were thankful to God for watching over them and for the Grace Missions donors for providing the opportunity to learn and grow.

———————

Ibrahima arrived in the States in mid-August. He had another wonderful visit. He gave talks at several churches, spent time learning new skills, continued to work on his English, and made many new friends. He stayed with several different families again, learning the variability of life in the US.

He brought two suitcases full of gifts and items for the auction. There were bracelets, necklaces, Dogon doors and statues, hand-woven and dyed textiles, and much more. Melissa and Josie went to work labeling and inventorying all of the items as the auction drew near.

When I asked Dennis Uecker what he remembers the most about Ibrahima's visit that summer, one story stood out: "We were at Rockhurst High School, and he was speaking to a group of young men about his passion for education and his quest to improve the lives of the students at Grace School. The Rockhurst young men had many questions about the life and circumstances of Ibrahima's Malian students, and they were sobered by his description of everyday life in Koro. Then one of them asked, 'What do you want most for your students?' Ibrahima's reply was, 'I want them to know Jesus.' Of all the answers he could have given, this was the window into his heart - and it impacted me greatly."

The Back to School event turned out better than we ever could have imagined. We nearly met our $60,000 goal, which was an incredible accomplishment for such an inexperienced, low budget group of fundraisers.

There were still some decisions that needed to be made as to the location of the school. It was great to be able to talk about them in person instead of piecemeal by text. Ibrahima had continued to negotiate with the landowners in the area. He had to be very careful to downplay his involvement with people from the US. That knowledge would at least double the price of the land.

Upon returning to Mali it took a few months before he accepted the fact that he wasn't going to get a better piece of land. The school would be three stories of three classrooms each as he had originally planned. The next step was to finalize the blueprints with his brother Zacharie and begin preparing the ground.

On December 6, 2013 a two-year-old boy named Emile Ouamouno died in southern Guinea. His mother, sister and grandmother all soon developed fever, vomiting and bloody stools before dying within weeks of Emile. It would be several months before he would be identified as "patient zero" of the massive Ebola outbreak in West Africa. By late March sixty-one people had died in the country and the first cases had been diagnosed in Liberia and Sierra Leone. Despite warnings from Doctors Without Borders (MSF) in April that this outbreak was unprecedented, the World Health Organization still called it relatively small.

In July, as deaths were at six hundred fifty and climbing rapidly, MSF called Ebola "out of control." It wasn't until August that the WHO declared the Ebola epidemic a "public health emergency of international concern."

In September, the death toll hit three thousand and there were sporadic cases in Nigeria, France, England and even the US. That month I traveled to Uganda with a large group of medical professionals for our yearly MMF mission. Although Uganda had a history of Ebola outbreaks, the current epidemic did not involve the country.

Fear of the disease reached a crescendo after our return to the states as containment measures didn't seem to be working in the three countries that were most affected. Quarantines, temperature checks at airports, calls to close US borders, massive and expensive Ebola training at hospitals across the country all added to the anxiety the disease was causing.

I was talking about Ebola at a conference being held at a local junior college in late October when we learned that a two-year-old child had died of the disease in Mali. Those of us that knew and loved the country felt our hearts sink. We prepared for the worst when we learned that the toddler had been sick and bleeding on a public bus traveling half way across Mali. The number of potential contacts was so high. And then later an Iman died of the disease and had a traditional funeral with a large amount of physical contact with his dead body.

As we held our breath and mourned for West Africa something miraculous happened. With border checks, airport screening and a massive education campaign, Mali health officials were able to contain the disease. We were forced to cancel our plans to return in January 2015 but thought there would be a chance of visiting sometime later in the year.

The incubation time of the Ebola virus is twenty-one days. If an exposed person hasn't developed symptoms within three weeks, they likely aren't going to. The CDC used twice that number, forty-two days, as the official cut off. Mali was declared disease-free on January 18th. A total of six deaths were reported in the country, still a tragedy but it certainly felt like a victory.

By late winter the overall number of new cases and deaths throughout West Africa had begun to slow and the media had moved on to other stories. In March the total number of deaths topped ten thousand, but new deaths were averaging a little more than a hundred a week. That was down from six hundred a week in December.

With that encouraging news, we decided to travel to Mali in April. It would be another small group. Two surgeons, two nurses, and four supporting people, including my thirteen-year-old son, Jackson, left for Bamako on April 11th.

It was the hottest and driest part of the year. Daytime temperatures were 108 degrees and the morning lows were still in the mid 80's. It was fairly brutal. We spent the night in Dagabo village, as had become our routine.

That year we ran a quick clinic for sexually transmitted diseases. STD's are a big problem in rural Mali as they are throughout the world. They cause painful symptoms and urethral stricture in men and can lead to cervical cancer in women. We treated all of the adults in the village with an injection and some pills and talked to them about how the diseases are spread. We encouraged fidelity and safety.

The clinic was very well received and was a good start for our small but enthusiastic group. As always, Ibrahima and Korotimi were our main translators. We moved to Dr. Oumar's clinic the next day and got right to work setting up the operating rooms, the pharmacy, the clinic spaces, and the pre and post-op areas. Tammy and I were operating by early afternoon.

We worked long hours with very little sleep for the next three days. There was no air conditioning in the operating room and opening the windows to the courtyard didn't seem to help, not to mention the fact that it was an invasion of privacy for the patients, so we kept them closed. We did our best to stay hydrated as the temperatures rose throughout the day. Even the metal on the OR tables felt scalding.

I finally had a chance to sit down with Ibrahima and catch up on the day of our departure. It was the first time that we had really talked since his visit to the US the previous summer. The fundraiser had helped our financial situation immensely. We now had enough money to begin construction on the school.

He explained that the first three classrooms would be built that year. He also added an administration building and three bathrooms (outhouses, basically) on to the plans. Going over the expenditures and budget, he had an additional request for a sound system with microphones to use for the big Student's Day celebration and other events.

I gave him tentative approval and said I would discuss all of the exciting developments and plans with the others upon my return. Our group had pizza and told stories for entirely too long at our usual spot in Bamako and then rushed to the airport, leaving Mali for the year after midnight.

———————————

By June of 2015, the bricks were being made to begin construction. There had been no rain for over six months so the wells were very dry. We talked about renting a truck to carry water from the Niger River, but the transportation costs were simply too high. So Ibrahima did what he always did, he improvised. He hired men to find water any way they could. They brought it by donkey cart in colorful five-gallon plastic jugs. Hundreds were required and it was a slow process.

By most measures the school year was a great success. Despite continued sporadic threats of violence and the fear of Ebola, parents kept their children in school. With money raised by Grace Missions they had textbooks for the first time, something that the public school children didn't have. They were learning practical skills as well as advancing their academic knowledge. And they did all of this while building a strong biblical foundation for their lives.

There were other big successes. Even though the severe drought continued, construction on the school was going well. Most of the bricks had been made and the bathrooms were constructed. The Student's Day was another hit. The children chose "peace" as the theme. As in Jesus Christ, Prince of Peace. In Ibrahima's words, "with many dances, songs, and more activities the kids displayed their thirst for peace in our country. They even claimed to be able to bring peace if they were given the responsibility to run the country." They also had ten student teachers during the last trimester. They all had chosen Grace as the location for their internship. The fresh ideas and energy were a pleasure to have in the classrooms.

Despite all of this, Ibrahima had worries about the ninth grade class. Many of the children had transferred in just for the second half of the year. He was concerned that because his teachers didn't have enough time with them that they would do poorly on the national exam. It turned out his fears were confirmed. There were twenty-seven in the grade but only four passed the DEF. This was a huge difference from prior years and although more in line with national averages, was a great disappointment for everyone.

The failure was something that Ibrahima and the teachers would have to carry with them for the next three months, until school started again. On one hand we wanted to reach as many people as possible with the gift of education and the Gospel. On the other, we wanted to properly prepare students for high school and life. Our prayer was that we could do both.

BRANDON POMEROY

Chapter 4
A Firm Foundation and Hope for Tomorrow

Ibrahima knew that there had been a change in the way that the DEF exam was calculated, but hadn't realized what an impact it would make on his students. In previous years, classwork had counted towards the final result. Starting with the June 2015 exam, only the test itself counted. He didn't feel it should have made that large of a difference to his students, but he resolved to discover new methods to ensure success the next year.

As the summer of 2015 progressed, the rain did finally come. At one point it rained over two inches in ninety minutes, filling the streets with water. The water pressure was enough on the freshly poured cement to destroy the new bathrooms. However the restoring rain was still celebrated, and construction resumed as soon as everything dried out.

Most of the construction workers were Muslim. During Ramadan, which stretched from mid-June to mid-July that year, the workers fasted all day so there was a slowdown in productivity. It picked up again afterwards and Ibrahima was hopeful that they would finish in time for the start of school in the fall.

With the well filled and a water pump in place, water was no longer an issue. In July it was the sand. It had been purchased in

Bandiagara but transportation costs were high and the number of trucks that were available to bring it was low. That time of year most trucks were busy hauling fertilizer and produce and it took several weeks to get the sand to the site.

By August the roof was in place. All that was left was to plaster the walls with concrete. Wood was used to prop up the ceiling and walls as they dried. It took a full three weeks to dry so it was a race against time to get the timber up before the last week of the month.

Zacharie had been instrumental in getting the building to that point, but he had to return to Bamako in early August. He left the finishing touches for Ibrahima to handle alone. Grace Missions supported Ibrahima the best we could with emails and texts, but communication remained difficult and sporadic.

In the meantime, we were working on expanding Grace Missions' reach. Leading up to the 2014 fundraising event we developed a blog and a Facebook account, but neither one was particularly active. Most communication went out in our emails on a more or less monthly basis. We felt that as the organization matured and grew that we needed to offer more timely information. We wanted to post more photographs and more frequent short updates.

We turned to Jonathan Klee from Perception Funding to give us a little push. Based in Belton, MO his organization helps Christian-based organizations become more sustainable by aiding with fundraising tips and with social media. We began talking with Jonathan in the summer of 2015. He gave us tremendous advice and helped get our website up and running.

We began growing our Facebook presence, and my daughter Sofia started an Instagram account for Grace. Ibrahima aided the increased online presence greatly. He still didn't have any kind of reliable Internet accessibility. No dial up, cable or Wi-Fi. What he did have, however, was a phone, and although it wasn't anything like what even the poorest person in the US has, he was able to send pictures and texts over a cellular connection.

It took several tries to get a picture to send, but by shrinking the file size by two-thirds he was more successful and we had beautiful images to share with our supporters. We tried to get at least two images out a week. It is difficult to picture what is going on in Koro, Mali for most people. It is so foreign and remote, and outside of our day-to-day concerns. The pictures help immensely to bring the place close. It makes it seem more real in many ways.

We needed to generate a little excitement and build momentum as the first three classrooms neared completion right before school began. We did this by creating a virtual fundraiser in which we updated our supporters and gave them an opportunity to contribute to the school. People are so busy and don't always have the time or energy for yet another Saturday evening fundraiser. By making it convenient and by involving as many people as we could, we were able to raise over $10,000, which was sorely needed to refill our capital fund. This also gave us a good jump on the capital required for the second set of classrooms.

The supporting timber was removed, the walls were painted, the floors were swept and the desks were arranged just in time for the first day of school. One classroom was split down the middle by a temporary barrier so that first and second grades could share. The third and fourth graders had their own rooms. Everyone was so excited about the new school. Even the middle schoolers in the rented building three blocks away enjoyed the extra space. They could spread out and not worry about the noise and disruption of the younger kids.

Some of the teachers were still part time, but as Ibrahima's experience as an administrator grew and as the teachers developed a longer track record, several became full time. He continued to help train student teachers and also brought more seasoned instructors from the public school to help out. One of the goals had always been to raise the overall quality of instruction in and around Koro, and Grace was doing just that.

———

We began to assemble a group of doctors, nurses, and support people to travel to Mali in January for our annual medical mission trip. The immediate threat of Ebola had faded away and we were generating more interest about the mission than we had in several years. We set up a meeting for one of the days after Thanksgiving to plan the details and to fill in the new people with what to expect.

Even though medical threats had lessened, violent ones continued to pop up. In August 2015 gunmen attacked a hotel in Sevare, killing a UN employee and four others. Things were quiet for a few months, but then in Paris on Friday, November 13th coordinated attacks at a soccer stadium, several restaurants, and a concert venue killed one hundred thirty people and injured more then three hundred fifty. ISIS claimed responsibility as revenge for military action in Syria and Iraq. There were signs that Belgium would be next.

The next Friday it was Mali's turn again. This time it was a much larger incident than the country had experienced before. Masked gunmen entered the Radisson Blu hotel in Bamako and began shooting people, eventually killing twenty before being killed themselves. It would be months before a somewhat clear picture of who planned the attack emerged. A member of the Islamic militant group Al Mourabitoun, an offshoot of Al Qaeda, was arrested in April 2016. It was apparently performed in retaliation of failing to meet demands of the group and their desire to have more autonomy in north Mali.

The incident, occurring about a week before we needed to finalize our trip to Mali, could not have come at a worse time. It worried most of us to the point that we decided to cancel the mission. Only Tammy, Abigail and I would travel to Mali this time. Also, our friend, local soccer star and Mali native Ibrahim Kante, would be there getting married to Fatima, whom he met in Kansas City. We wanted to be sure to show him support by traveling to Bamako if at all possible.

Grace Missions ran a quick Giving Tuesday campaign after Thanksgiving to raise money for medications that I would bring to Koro. Intestinal worms and schistosomiasis are very common pathogens in areas with poor sanitation and access to clean water. They are a major cause of absenteeism from school and work, and over the long term can even lead to death in various different ways. One tablet each of albendazole and praziquantel treats both diseases and helps prevent infection for several months. We had treated all children and most adults with albendazole at Dr. Oumar's clinic for several years. The idea for treating schistosomiasis came during research for my novel that fall. Both are very cost effective interventions. Several kind friends of Grace Missions donated the money, and we put in the order to pick up the medications in Mali.

The three of us flew out on New Year's Eve and rang in the New Year somewhere over the Atlantic Ocean. Following the usual confusion and delays, we finally got to our beds for the night after three. Ibrahim Kante has a large family that lives in Bamako. I stayed with his brother Aloo and the ladies stayed with Omar.

The next morning we visited Kante's mother on the other side of Bamako. We sat and talked and waited for things to

65

happen, a common pastime in Mali, as time travels at a different speed there. By early afternoon Ibrahima arrived with his brother Zacharie and the three of us took off in the direction of Koro. The plan was for us to meet up with Tammy and Abby in Ouelessebougou in four days to run a brief surgical clinic with Dr. Oumar. They would attend Ibrahim and Fatima's wedding and then spend the remaining time in Dagabo village.

We spent the first night in San, which was past Segou but well before Mopti, arriving after dark. We stayed in a very simple but clean and safe motel. The next morning after a breakfast of bread, butter, jam and tea we headed east. Following a short detour into Mopti for lunch and to buy Timbuktu salt for Ibrahima's father's animals, we drove deeper into Dogon country. We got to Koro by about five in the afternoon, just in time to look at the school before darkness fell.

It was amazing to see the school through Zacharie's eyes. He hadn't been to the site in about six months and was excited to be able to tour it. He looked at the foundation, the bathrooms, the roof, and the walls. He measured things and put a level on different areas. He was clearly pleased with the way it looked. Zacharie doesn't speak English and Ibrahima had been translating the past two days, but he didn't need words to tell me what he thought. He said it would certainly hold two more floors, that the foundation had been prepared properly.

The next morning after an egg, fresh bread, and tea, we visited the school at both locations. With the teachers' help, the medicine was distributed to the middle school kids. I talked to them and answered questions about the US. I was the first white person they had seen in their town in years, certainly the first one to visit their school, and they were shy and inquisitive at the same time. They asked about my family and about computers. I was able to interview a few as well.

The children all drew a picture using the construction paper and crayons that I brought with me. It was interesting to see what they created. Many drew their homes. There were intricate flowers and the Malian flag. Some of the boys drew motorcycles or cars just like kids back home. Many used their pencils rather than crayons and pulled out protractors and rulers to make precise lines.

Three of the older boys carried my suitcases that were full of gifts, supplies, and medicines for the kids through the dusty roads to the new building. The place was alive with the sound of children. In each classroom, a student was standing at the chalkboard writing something and reciting their lesson. It was so organized. The enthusiastic and attentive hum of the students, the teachers' focus, and the still cool interior of the classrooms that morning was all extremely impressive. This could just as easily have been a class in a wealthy school district in the US.

The younger children all cooperated just as well as the older ones as they dutifully swallowed the medicine. Ibrahima had notified all of the parents of the upcoming treatment, giving them a chance to opt out. Something for which I was thankful. His trips to schools in Kansas and Missouri have taught him the importance of involving parents in their children's education.

I answered a few questions for the younger kids as well. They were all presented with a toothbrush and instructions for proper brushing. I talked to them about the importance of school and listening to their teachers.

They surprised me with a beautiful hymn. Their loud voices were accentuated with clapping that was remarkably rhythmic and on the beat as the final verse approached. I could feel the pride that the children and teachers had in their school. In their small, poor, remote town, they have the opportunity to learn and grow in a safe, loving, modern environment. Their eyes are opening to the wider world and to their place in it. They are learning that life is about giving rather than taking, about sharing and working together so that all are lifted up.

Ibrahima's daughter Catherine is in the first grade. One of the reasons that he started Grace School was to have a place where his children could have an outstanding education in a Christian environment. Five years later he is able to walk a few blocks and see Catherine learning and growing. She comes home each day with new knowledge. Like all parents he is proud and protective, happy to see her grow up and yet sad that she no longer needs him quite as much.

She is definitely a big sister, pulling Louise's arm to get her to come to bed and helping her mom with baby sister Ruth. She is smart and assertive. The other two girls are equally beautiful. Ruth's eyes were so wide as she watched me carefully. She had never seen such a thing and wasn't immediately enamored with me, but she did eventually loosen up and smile. Louise was happy to see her uncle Zacharie and sat with us as we ate a wonderful dinner prepared by Rachel.

The visit to Koro was entirely too short, but being able to see the place was a gift to me. I could now clearly picture what has been accomplished and what still needs to be done. The school needs electricity. The line is only about a hundred feet away but Ibrahima is still negotiating with the city to get it to the school. A new school sign, a fourth wall to the perimeter fence, and a more reliable source of water are all on the to-do list as well.

After visiting Grace School Tuesday morning we returned to Ibrahima's house for lunch. Rachel had plates, forks, and wine glasses set out on a tiny table in their living space in front of the sofa. Like she had the evening before, she brought in the covered metal bowls from the fire outside and laid them on the floor next to the table. She then went back outside to eat with the many children that stayed there. Ibrahima told me that he and Rachel typically ate together inside, but the culture dictated that the men eat alone when there is company.

Prior to the first meal the three of us shared together that week Ibrahima asked me to pray. By now we had a routine. This time it was Zacharie's turn and he prayed in French. I understood "Jesu" and "Dieu" and not a lot more but it was still beautiful. My previous trips to Mali had always been mainly medical and although there certainly were spiritual moments, we hadn't prayed openly. It felt nice to be able to share these intimate meals, to pray together, and to experience a little of the home lives of my friends.

The food consisted of soft, doughy bread over which we poured a thin onion gravy. Ibrahima said the gravy was made with Maggi, which is very common there. There were boiled beets to go along with it. Rachel also brought out large individual salads. The lettuce had been washed with a bleach solution. There were tomatoes and hard-boiled eggs as well, all tossed in a light oil and vinegar dressing. She had even purchased four one-liter boxes of mango juice for me. I had trouble convincing the brothers to share the juice with me but they eventually did.

It was a feast, a wonderful, unexpected meal that was a true gift. We were really trying to get out of town. The deadline was that Ibrahima wanted me to climb up a sheer wall that led to the plateau above the cliff villages where he was born. I was unclear how far away this was but knew that it became completely and suddenly dark at about six thirty and it was already a little past noon. Regardless, once we sat down, prayed, laughed, talked and ate, time seemed to slow down and my anxiety level uncharacteristically dropped a little bit.

Following the meal, I talked to the school kids that were staying with Ibrahima. There were usually fifteen people living in his tiny house. His family of five plus around ten students all shared the same outhouse and bucket shower. There were also three pigs, several chickens and a donkey in the small enclosed yard. I took pictures and accepted more gifts before saying a sad goodbye.

When we finally left, we tried to make up for lost time, hurrying out of town for about five minutes. But immediately upon turning from the main road to a small dirt one, we had to stop. Ibrahima greeted a man pushing a motorcycle. His two small daughters were walking alongside. After talking for a few minutes he continued on his way and the two girls were transferred to the back seat of the pickup. The motorcycle had a flat tire. The man would push it to the next village for repair and we would deliver the girls home. Ibrahima vaguely knew the villager and assured me that his home wasn't far out of the way.

We sped across the dirt. At times several tracks went off in different directions. Most of the drive was on a single donkey/bicycle/motorcycle trail with no indication of previous four wheeled vehicles. The two girls sat in the back smiling broadly as they rode in cool comfort.

As we bounced along, they began to nod. Thirty minutes later, when we had reached the village the older girl awakened and vomited extravagantly all over the back. The younger girl pointed to her mud brick home just as the odor began to overpower us. Their grateful and surprised mother helped us clean the truck as the villagers gathered to catch up with Ibrahima and Zacharie and to greet the pale visitor.

I discovered that the next-door neighbor was a pastor and that the small nondescript hut next to us was a church. Even in this Muslim country there are a surprising number of Christians. They worship in homes, in a few large churches and in simple buildings like the one that we had stumbled upon.

When the pastor opened up the church it took my breath away. It had a dirt floor, mud brick benches, three simple crosses molded onto the wall behind the altar, and the altar itself, formed from mud and covered with a white cloth. There was a poster of the Immaculate Heart of Mary partially covering the crosses. He showed me the drums and shakers that were used during worship. He told me that women sat on the right and men on the left and that the right side was full every Sunday.

I sat on the left for a few moments, Ibrahima and Zacharie quietly sitting beside me. I remember the stillness, the coolness of the bench, the comfort I felt in the midst of a long journey, the holiness of the place. Rising to leave, thanking the pastor, saying goodbye to the villagers gathered outside the church, I could feel the commonality, the grace and fellowship that would follow us throughout the week. There was a loving spark of spirit that is within us that radiated from all that we met.

When we arrived at Ibrahima's parent's village it was about three thirty. He actually clarified that it wasn't large enough to be a village, rather it was a small collection of families. His parents, his sister Suzanne and her family, and his brother Moses all lived there. There was a large group of children pounding millet on front of the home. Ibrahima's mom, Louisa, was in constant motion. She was making us a meal, swatting a goat, instructing the millet pounders, talking to her children, and finding gifts for us.

By the time she was finished, I had been given a large handful of unshelled peanuts that they had farmed, then a large canvas bag of peanuts, then a plastic bag of some kind of fruit that had been picked and dried, then a piece of Dogon artwork that I am certain was taken down from somewhere in their simple home, and then a dark blue woven blanket with an intricate pattern printed on the front. Among other things, Zacharie, who hadn't visited his parents in over a year, received a huge canvas bag of tamarind and another of peanuts. Ibrahima said that whenever he brought his parents something- a solar lantern, a big bag of rice, a pot for cooking or for storage- he could be sure that it would be

71

gone the next time he visited. They were forever giving things away.

Even though we had eaten a large meal only three hours before, Louisa had prepared food for us and I knew that we couldn't refuse. She had someone carry three chairs into a clean empty hut. Once we were seated she brought in two metal bowls and set them on the floor between us. One contained a macaroni- type dish with a tomato sauce, and the other contained what appeared to be chicken in some kind of sauce. She brought a bucket of water to wash our hands. There were no utensils so after a prayer from Ibrahima we just dug in. I didn't eat the meat but did enjoy the savory, soft pasta.

Once again not knowing what was next, I ate too much. She brought a bowl of millet porridge flavored with sugar and what Zacharie thought was tamarind although it could have been baobab fruit. We drank from a shared, green plastic ladle. It was so sweet, rich and filling. Realizing that the kids outside had ground the millet made it taste that much better. There was also coffee. It had so much milk and sugar in it that I couldn't really taste any coffee but it was delicious as well.

We were there less than an hour. Again we took pictures, exchanged a few stories and then had to get on our way towards the cliff dwellings. It was a beautiful place and I was sorry to leave. There were trees, some grass, and even pretty green birds that could have been parrots flying from branch to branch. And I felt so welcomed by the Kodio family.

We finally made it to the base of the cliff at about five in the early evening. We were able to drive along the narrow road that connected the tiny villages. Parking at one of them, Ibrahima and I got out, while Zacharie said he would meet us at the top. He drove away and the two of us began climbing up the rock wall. It appeared to be several hundred feet high and I couldn't see a path, but there were ancient mud structures all along the escarpment.

I followed behind Ibrahima, carefully watching where I put my feet, balancing myself with my hands and occasionally slipping a little as we made our way up and up. Ibrahima walked backwards as he narrated and pointed the way. He never once touched the rocks with his hands. He had been on this path hundreds of times and it was like a suburban sidewalk to him.

He showed me places where grain offerings were made on the rocks, some small clay idols, and pointed out different huts that had special uses. It had been several years since tourists had come this way and the few villagers that we passed were very interested in me. They stopped and talked to Ibrahima, usually remembering him and his family as he explained what we were doing there. They always left with a big smile.

When we made it to the top Zacharie was waiting with the truck. A huge crowd of laughing and screaming children were there to greet us as well. They had heard that a Toubab (white person) was coming and they were beyond excited. We got in the pickup and drove a mile or two to Sangha, where we would spend the night.

We stayed in the old missionary house. It was now owned by the Dogon Church and Ibrahima had arranged for us to sleep there. The caretaker brought us yet another meal and fired up the generator to give us light and electricity to charge our phones. He even helped Zacharie change a tire that had succumbed to the rocky roads.

The following morning we toured the small village, Ibrahima showing me where he had grown up, the big, beautifully constructed church where he had worshiped, the homes of old friends. We stopped in to visit a few people, their eyes opening widely as they recognized Zacharie, who hadn't visited in years.

We couldn't stay long, however, and soon were on our way back to Bamako. We stopped in Bandiagara to repair our tire and ran into the head of the district's church. He had visited Grace School before and had very good things to say about it. He praised Ibrahima and I could feel how important his support was to my friend.

We finally arrived back to Bamako several hours after dark. An uncharacteristic January rainstorm added some additional excitement to the drive, but we made it safely.

The next morning, we drove to Ouelessebougou and caught up with Tammy and Abby who had arrived about an hour before. We quickly began setting up the operating rooms and unpacking our supplies. The anesthesiologist had arrived from Bamako that morning as well. He had assisted us the year prior. He was hard working and quite competent.

Tammy and I screened patients as Ibrahima, Korotimi, and a few others helped with translation. By three in the afternoon we were operating and we didn't stop until noon the next day. I was able to steal about an hour of sleep at about four in the morning but Tammy went straight through. We ended with a four-hour procedure to repair a gigantic abdominal hernia. The patient was very sweet and we felt obligated to help. We had to resect some bowel as there was a huge amount of scar tissue, but in the end everything came together nicely.

After packing up the things we couldn't leave behind, we hurried back to Bamako, cleaned up, ate at our usual pizza place, and got to the airport in the nick of time. We said our bittersweet goodbyes and returned to the reality of our lives once again.

———————

After allowing myself to reacclimatize a little, I met with the others from Grace Missions, filling them in on the trip. We looked at our financial picture and were pleased to find that we had enough money to begin the second set of classrooms. We also calculated that tuition paid by the student's families had supplied 25% of our operating expenses. It wasn't the 50% that has been our ultimate goal but it was still encouraging. Although we don't believe that the school can be self-sufficient anytime soon, we do want to keep expenses at a sustainable level.

As the spring semester progressed we received occasional updates from Ibrahima. The seasonal drought continued, slowing construction as bricks were made. He spent time supervising the workers as well as helping run the school.

One day in April, smoke began billowing towards the school. In Ibrahima's words, "Masons, technicians, workmen ran to help the family overcome a blazing fire in the grass hut in front of their living quarters. There was very little chance of success in fighting this fire if the construction team was not there with such a large quantity of water. It was a great relief to the family. Two powerless kids were in the house while the door was on fire. Their mother was outside and couldn't help and their dad was away."

He continued, "This fire could have happened to us when we were in the grass walled classrooms. It is such a blessing that we are now out of this hazardous situation, that we are freed from these risks." He understood better than anyone the many miracles that had occurred over the years.

Even the existence of the small well that was being used for drinking water and to make bricks was a miracle. Ibrahima said in a letter that spring, "While city construction projects starve, at Grace we have water from a relatively shallow well to continue the building. Some families get drinking water from us. We would like to continue sharing with them as long as they have the need and we have the water."

Another small grace was the students' health. Usually by late spring, many children miss school because of intestinal diseases. Dehydration and pain make them too weak to concentrate or even walk to school. Ibrahima noticed that not one student had been absent that semester from diarrheal diseases. He attributed it to the medicines that they had taken at the beginning of the year. Such a small action had led to a wonderful return.

It has been a tremendous journey. One in which scores of children and their families have already been positively affected. Girls that can clearly see a future. Boys whose dreams have grown. Bibles are being read. Community is being created. And the world is becoming a little kinder, a little smaller. Ibrahima Kodio has said many times that there is no way a book could be written about him or about Grace School. And every time I tell him the same thing- this book has already been written. It was written on the stars. It was written on the hearts of everyone involved. Someone just needed to get it down on paper.

Acknowledgements

The author wishes to thank the following people for their support and encouragement on this project:

The Ueckers- Josh, Josie, Dennis and Judy, without whom there would be no Grace Missions. Ibrahima and Rachel Kodio, without whom there would be no Grace School. Tammy Neblock-Beirne, Abigail Hayo, Sophie O'Neal, Pepper Card, and all of my other Mali heroes and travel buddies over the years. The many churches and organizations that have supported Grace Missions. Jeanne Smith, whose insight and memories were invaluable. Zacharie Kodio for his humility and brave driving skills. Dr. Oumar and all of the staff and translators at Clinique Paix in Ouelessebougou. The hospitality of Boi Doumbia and his family. My friend and sounding board, Jamie Langston. And Lucie, Sofia, and Jackson Pomeroy for allowing me the freedom to travel, to write and to dream.

About Elpida Press

In our busy lives, when we are only able to see things superficially and quickly, when information comes in headlines and sarcastic quotes, when everything seems fragmented and temporary, and when our actions are motivated by fear rather than hope, Elpida Press provides an alternative. A non-profit publishing company unsatisfied with the status quo, we are committed to love and reconciliation. We are on the lookout for skilled artists and writers to work with. As a non-profit we are also dependent on your kind donations. Every little bit helps as we strive to be part of the solution, carefully mending and repairing what has been nearly torn apart.

Please visit our website and follow us on Facebook.

Elpidapress.org
Facebook.com/elpidapress

Also by **Brandon Pomeroy**

"A spiritually thought provoking and thoroughly engaging novel."
-Newell Williams, President of Brite Divinity School at
Texas Christian University

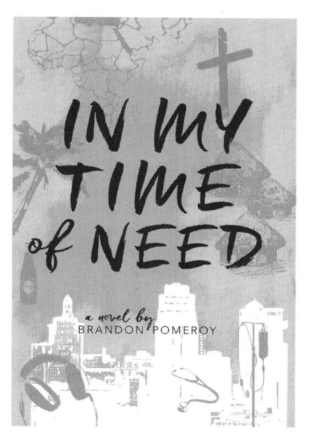

In My Time of Need is an unconventional love story that takes
the reader from Kansas City to Central America and East
Africa. Filled with grace and humor, it is a spiritual journey
that is as universal as it is meaningful.

Available now at Elpidapress.org and Amazon.com

About Grace Missions Inc.

Grace Missions improves educational opportunities for children in Mali, Africa and provides a Biblical foundation to their lives by sharing our abundance with those that have very little. We provide hope and confidence for a better tomorrow. We feel that education with a Biblical foundation is the key to a hopeful future, a lasting peace, and personal fulfillment in developing countries.

Thank you for purchasing this book. To learn more about Grace Missions and to donate as we continue to support these wonderful children, visit our website and follow us on Facebook and Instagram.

Gracemissionskc.org
Facebook.com/gracemissionsmali

Made in the USA
Lexington, KY
19 July 2018